To Deb —

With love from
Joan & Rube.
6 / June / 2017.

Pat Lee

Nudge the Morning

With a foreword by John Miles

Acknowledgements

Some of the poems in this collection have appeared,
not necessarily in identical form, in the following publications:
Friendly Street Poets Readers 2013, 2014, 2015, 2016;
InDaily Poets Corner, SA; *Studio*, NSW;
The Write Angle, Queensland; *The Mozzie*, Queensland;
Valley Micropress, NZ.

Dedicated to my family and friends

I acknowledge that I live on the land of the Kaurna people,
the traditional owners and custodians
of what we now call the Adelaide plains.

Nudge the Morning
ISBN 978 1 76041 311 8
Copyright © text Pat Lee 2017
Cover image and internal illustrations: Catherine Kite

First published 2017 by
GINNINDERRA PRESS
PO Box 3461 Port Adelaide 5015 Australia
www.ginninderrapress.com.au

Contents

Foreword   11

sitting in the morning…   15

Days   17
Norinna Herd at Harrogate   18
I Caught the Moon   19
The Undercliff Walk   20
The Anvil Cloud   21
Two Summers   22
The Owls   23

run run…   25

coming of age   27
Boy on the Platform   28
Travel notes   29
New Boy   30
Run Run   31
Monochrome Commuters   32
Girl in a Strawberry Dress   33
Woman down the Street   34
Cats   35
Keeping Track   36
8 a.m. Bus   37
Quality Time   38

those who want to see will wait…   39

Mount Lofty Ranges   41
Purple Whisperings   42
Adelaide Snapshots   43
At the Traffic Lights   44
Man with a Bare Back   45
Winter Car Park   46

Lemons in Boxes 47
Talk about Trees 48
Brave New Street 51
Pie's Spot 52
Staffy 53
The Fox 54
Victor Harbor 55
Barossa Spring 56
Didgeridoo and Mukkuri Music 58

days of green... 59
As a Goldfinch Sang with Clear Notes 61

from a train window... 69
Tides Beneath the Bridge 71
G8 Summit 2008, Lake Tōya 72
Kobe Autumn Days 73
Autumn 74
Glimpses of Spring 75
Cherry Blossoms 76
Speed Reading 77
Rosebay Willow Herb 78
A Visit to Stanley 79
O washi 80
Fjord Land 81

earth to earth, ashes to ashes, dust to dust... 83
Hot 85
Summer 86
Koalas in the Heat 87
Little Grassbird 88
Dinner 89
Southern Sunset 90
Cyclone Yasi's Reach 91

Evensong at Beecher's Brook 92
Three Gums 93
The Bridge 94

ebb and flow... 95

Shadows 97
Burgess Hill Woman 98
Yesterday 100
One December Afternoon 101
Silky Oak 102
Briefcase 103
Today's Tide 104
My Humbling Days 105
Horizon Line 106
The Forest 107

Author's note 108

our place in the universe, the past and the present,
our future with birdsong, silence or thunder,
our fears and hopes, our restless and calm…

'Didgeridoo and Mukkuri Music'

Foreword

On first reading Pat Lee's poetry I was faced with a dilemma. A half dozen poems, sent hopefully for one to be chosen for *InDaily*'s Poet's Corner. Dilemmas, though, as with Gordian knots, can be easily solved.

I reread the poems, but it is always that first reading that tells what is intuitively seen – as to whether you are dealing with a natural poet or not. 'I can't choose,' I formed my reply. 'We'll cut the knot. All will have to be to accepted. Bear with things in getting them into the column over time.'

It is said that poetry is an art form, so as with all art forms it must have its craft and technique. Imagery, simile and metaphor, rhythm, stress and meter and more, all if the poet is good enough, juxtapose to give us poetry that would read, speak and sound right, be poetry that is simply good poetry. Good poetry, from device and means that are mastered through time and work, practised by the practitioner until he or she is indeed their master.

But as skilled as poets and their work may that way become, there is another aspect so importantly required in the defining of the complete poet – the separating of substance from just style. Bitter-sweetly in a way, it is the one that cannot be learnt, for it is the natural one.

'Near' and 'far', the two different aspects were called as long ago as in Geoffrey Chaucer's time, though even then the debate about them was old. The nearness, the familiar, of the conscious craft, as opposed to the otherwise farness of a 'subconscious' other. Acquired skill or inborn talent; nurture vs nature; practised method, or that sublime essence called Inspiration by the Muse.

More recently than Chaucer, South Australia's own Paul Pfeiffer, an original force of the internationally renowned Angry Penguin movement in Australian poetic Modernism, put it that, yes, craftsmanship or technique were as important to the poet as they were to the musician, painter or sculptor, but that there also had to be something else, again to make the natural poet. 'The gift' were Pfeiffer's own words for it, that intangible something with many names, one of them once again simply being inspiration.

Ninety per cent to ten per cent, our two aspects are said to be. Ninety per cent the perspiration, ten per cent the inspiration. How important that ninety per cent is, once more is not to be understated. Of equal importance, though, despite its lesser volume, is the ten per cent.

Nudge the Morning is a collection of poetry I found to be not only of the ninety per cent, but also fully of the ten. It is the poem collection of the natural poet. Throughout there is a lyricism and landscaping from a once more pastoral time, mixed seamlessly with those of today's both urban and urbane one. Chosen word and inspired thought throughout the poems, all accompany any mastery of those crafts and techniques.

'Evensong at Beecher's Brook', 'The Owls', 'Lemons in Boxes', 'Brave New Street', 'Winter Car Park', 'Barossa Spring' were those first six poems I saw of Pat Lee's. They are all here, along with many more of the same vigour and outright pleasure to read. Together they make up a collection of poems that are as diverse in subject matter as they are alike in feeling and expressive energy. Titling, that can be a hugely neglected art in itself these days, alone draws the reader to each poem. Not that there is just reliance there on our crafts and techniques once again. Rather is it that each title speaks straight out for its poem, turns out to be but a fully fledged reflection of the poem's own such strengths.

Successful observation is also an integral part of the natural poet. Successful, in that how the subject has been seen by the poet is how it is conveyed to the reader. It is information vs interpretation. Lee does succeed, and to say that I have not met Lee is true, but then I have, by this way and others through her poetry.

Nudge the Morning starts with an epigraph, from the poem 'Didgeridoo and Mukkuri Music':

> our place in the universe, the past and the present,
> our future with bird song, silence or thunder,
> our fears and hopes, our restless and calm.

The first lines of the first poem, 'Days', are

> Days walk in and out of my life
> leaving their footprints behind

The last lines of the last poem, 'The Forest, Kuitpo', are

> a sense of something great and good
> in this gilded green cathedral.

Such clarity and directness of idea are unbroken throughout the collection. True conveyance to the reader is achieved. It is for these so 'far' of reasons that Lee's poetry succeeds, on a level that all crafting and other, no matter how mastered, could not take it to alone.

John Miles, Adelaide, January 2017

sitting in the morning…

Days

Days walk in and out of my life
leaving their footprints behind.

Sitting in the morning
on the edge of expecting something
I almost stopped myself
from walking into another day…

but wondered what its footprint might be.

Norinna Herd at Harrogate

I miss the breath of velvet-nostrilled afternoons
standing on the hill, warm within the grazing herd,
their mantras soothing in the air around.

Those Sunday afternoons,
chances to look beyond
impending days of drudge
locked in another week's relentless pace.
To see on clear days the far-off Goolwa lakes,
and ease into that calming distance,
where hours dissolve in shades of blue
and whisper in the wind,

There is no time, future or past,
from star dust, to star dust,
ends are beginnings.

See,
as evening mist curls close of day
along the valley floor
a new born calf stands for the first time.

What time is it?
It's now, it's always now.

I Caught the Moon

I caught the moon, just before I went to bed,
moving quietly between the Knox Cottage gums,
sliding between leaves and branches,
across the sky and past our home.

I caught the moon in the pantry window,
peering into neighbours' gardens,
turning shadows into mysteries.

I caught the moon silently doing her thing
when no one else was watching.

I caught the moon.

The Undercliff Walk

Peacehaven, England

From Greenwich Meridian Monument,
sharp-down, steep-slide, past nesting gulls
and wretched wind-worn weeds
snatching meagre space in chalky cracks,
down, down to the Undercliff Walk
built to withstand the weather of waves.

Smooth rounded by splash 'n' swash of sea
above, thud dull and slap of waves,
murmuring choruses of pebbles.

Slip, slide, sharp-down, steep-slide, chalk cliffs,
to run or walk and nod the polite hello,
all rhythmic with the slap 'n' swash of waves.
Or sit, to stare and think on France,
and watch while round the east headland
channel ferries come and go.

Sunbursts lacquering a rolling sea.
Seagulls soaring on upward draughts,
screech above the pebbles' chant.

Slip, slide, sharp-down, steep-slide, chalk cliffs
to face the wind and catch the slight spray air
and in some way feel part of
the ceaseless, salty aeons.

While gulls cry loud and pebbles chant low,
the waves, the waves, always the waves,
the ever slap 'n' swash,
down, down on the undercliff walk.

The Anvil Cloud

City to Bay Run, Adelaide to Glenelg

From the foreshore,
gazing west beyond the waves
for a moment, curved within the orb of sea,
balanced on horizon's edge:
an anvil cloud.

Not with the towering majesty
of an impending storm,
but pastel calm, almost translucent,
stretched long against the morning sky,
and for that moment, lingered longer,
to watch white sails breeze across the early day.

In the minute you arrived
within the second of a sigh,
or the time it takes to smile,
it slipped from the horizon,
leaving behind an empty sky.

With you,
I could not share what I had seen
gazing west beyond the waves
for there was only blue;
and I wondered in that moment,
if the thousand others waiting,
chanced to see it too.

Two Summers

We walked into summer that afternoon,
drawn to the cool lawn
and in the lull of the garden
lost in loving, our first child began
under the Poor Man's Orange tree.
High perched, and resplendent
Ramdas observed, then flew down,
fanned out his train for the sun
and shimmered iridescent.
Conceived late summer, our son; born late spring.

Two summers passed and on the third,
in the heat and folds of night,
on Egyptian white cotton we fell into loving,
then comma curled, me small-rounded in your arms,
embryonic our shape as a new life stirred within.
Conceived in midsummer, our second son;
born mid-spring.

With each birth, a clutch of chicks appeared
from a nest scratched together
in the same corner of our garden,
and I have often wondered why
Ramdas and Rena,
our neighbour's peacocks, hatched chicks
only when our sons were born.

The Owls

Ninox boobook

Over tangled dead wood, tucked with cobwebs
veils of green conceal their world.
Here they sit side by side or apart,
one up, one down and yet together,
snoozing nod-eyed, closed-eyed sleep,
or wondrous, round-eyed, winking.
Some days perched in the pittosporum they merge
with mottled leaves almost unseen, half hid,
watching us watching them
through the living room window.

Quiet, and at one with the garden's heartbeat
they ignore the daily chatter and din:
menacing mynahs' scratching shrieks,
bobbing blackbirds' anxious alarms,
and the tiresome twitters of tits.

As evening's blush folds into gold, day's azure
deepening to lapis, they preen and stretch,
featherly-fluffed as one they kiss,
and move apart in readiness.
No flicker, flinch or eyelash wink,
a sudden silent drop –
they fly away on a velvet wingbeat.

Distinct from our timed world
of wake-up alarms and always-bells,
telling us we are due or overdue
to go and do, be and get,
they appear when early light tinges the east.
Beige and brown, they simply merge with mottled leaves
as we rise to meet the tin rhythm of our next day.

run run...

coming of age

it's not a date it's a journey
in a minuscule space in time
from first breath until last
each step
each left or right turn
every lesson every understanding
a preparation for that final

coming of age

Boy on the Platform

Japan, Culture Day Holiday, 2014

On the busy platform,
a little boy,
stood behind the yellow line
waving a small brown towel.

He wiped his eyes
with the towel
and waved again.

Tears welled.
His mother bent to comfort him.
Without response,
he wiped his eyes
and waved the towel,
again and again.

Departure music sounded.
As the silent Shinkansen
slid out of the station
an old man returned to his seat,
and dried his eyes.

Travel notes

India, Bombay, January 1975
square platform with wheels
hands in worn thongs
withered legs,
crawling hair
the boy
asked me for money.

India, Calcutta, January 1975
shop doorway
worn step
thin boy
cupped hands
rice grains
floor swept.

Egypt, Cairo, February 1976
in a park
a little girl
used the space
behind a tree
as a toilet
an older boy
perhaps her brother
wiped her clean with leaves.

New Boy

First day at a posh private

a new bike
standard model

a new school bag
placed inside a woven basket
strapped to the back of his bike

a canary yellow helmet
matching reflective vest
trouser clips

on the road there
excited anticipation

on the road home
wishing his first day was his last.

Run Run

Run quickly through straight days.
Run hard down streets without a curve.
Run, run down treeless avenues
without places to pause and ponder,
where you can rest a while and watch
dawn's rays dance on dewy grass,
spiders weave in air,
fledglings flap from branch to branch
and sunset gild the clouds floating
between today and tomorrow.

Monochrome Commuters

They do not know the seasons,
or the wind's changing moods
across the day.
They do not see the sun at noon,
but rest and rise in the dark.

From underground,
with downward eyes,
between a city's concrete shadows,
absorbed, they text,
they move and miss:
the flowering weed in a wall,
pecking pigeons, scrappy sparrows.

No time to see or hear,
the autumnal rustle of colours,
the sound of falling shadows.

Monochrome commuters work
then choose to play in cyberspace:
charmed by the trite,
gripped by the vicious.

Always winter people –
monochrome commuters.

Girl in a Strawberry Dress

9 p.m. train, Victoria Station to Gatwick, England

White spots, strawberries and leaves
patterned her black halter-neck dress;
tight waist, flared skirt, skimming
crimson court shoes on bare feet.
Straight, henna coloured hair,
and a fringe of one tight curl
outlined her face;
eyebrows pencilled cherry brown,
copious black eyeliner, Cleopatra-like,
flushed cheeks, snub nose and scarlet lips.
Arms and back sunburnt.

The new husband, with a crew cut,
wore an orange shirt and reflective glasses.
His belly bulged over his jeans.
His parrot-beak nose sat above thick lips.
He spluttered when he spoke – loudly.
He talked a lot.

From little bottles they poured champagne
into plastic cups. The more they drank
the louder he got, the more she giggled.
First leg of our honeymoon, she told everyone.

The tepid middle-aged couple opposite
opened up their newspapers and held them high.

Woman down the Street

It seemed by all accounts
her disposition
was
like a row of steel spikes
stuck
on a window ledge,
warning,
Do not try to land.
She
lived alone.

Cats

They don't have to:
wait for the right moment
put things, that shouldn't be important, first
lead lives complicated by the whims of the world.

They can:
stretch in the sun, lie in the shade,
claim the padded chair,
purr themselves into a curl,
grow old with grace,
and if lucky, die with dignity.

Keeping Track

When days walk you through weeks
and you do not remember
where you've been,
and you cannot see
where you are going
and you rush through,
knocking and bumping
the weekend against the clock,
and go to work on Monday

where do the years go?

8 a.m. Bus

Hove to Brighton, England

Apart from the scarf with white flecks
she was dressed in black, woolly beanie
pulled down hard, heavy handbag bulging.

She clambered onto the bus,
dropped onto on a flip-up seat,
positioned four fat shopping bags under her legs,
scrabbled in a pocket for her mobile phone.
Escaped from under the beanie,
ginger curls softened her thin freckled face.
As she gazed at the pelting rain, her mobile rang.

Don't worry, Dad, I'm on my way.
No, Dad, I haven't got Mum with me.

The bus swayed.
A bag's contents tumbled out.
A tin rolled across the floor.
Head bent to one side, ear on phone,
wedged between chin and shoulder,
she started retrieving.

Yes, yes, Dad, that's right.
Mum won't be coming home from hospital.
No, Dad, no, the kids aren't with me,
I've just put them on the bus for school.

Quality Time

When does this happen,
at what hour of the day
or time in your life?

do you have to book in?

those who want to see will wait...

Mount Lofty Ranges

I know I'm home, when I see them,
from the plane window
old, worn and rounded, the Mount Lofty Ranges,
stretched north to south on a long narrow plain.

West side of the ranges, sage green, deep viridian
overlook the city, then across Gulf St Vincent
to the vast Southern Ocean.
Precious rain drops when clouds rise over their soft curves
often falling short, surrendered to sea.

East side, dry grass, rain shadow country
with granite boulders balanced on hillsides
gradually weathering in frost, sun and wind,
and views to a distance like sky never ending
over a sparse plain, but for the meandering
Murray's thin ribbon of green,
then beyond toward rock and rust desert sand.

My link with the hills is less than a flicker,
my forebears, among the first hills settlers
came with a will to prosper, be free.
From their stories I gain courage.
From the hills I draw strength.

But the original inhabitants, the Peramangk people,
lived wise with this landscape, their traditional lands;
understood the spirits, the sounds, light and colours
of creeks, valleys and forests,
knew the contours and crevices, the secrets of caves,
their connections profound…

Purple Whisperings

Against peeling paint of long-standing verandas,
scraggy brown of brush fences,
and sharp lines of corrugated iron,
discreetly over clinker brick walls,
corner-tucked then twined round drainpipes,
over and along branches of just budding trees,
tracings of wisteria.
Languid falls of wistful, powdery, purple
gently displacing winter, quietly beckoning spring.

How easy is it not to see, what is so quickly gone,
arriving without a loud shout, or fanfare of
bright colour, but only purple whisperings.

Too soon honey-green leaves displace
the tranquil haze and long, waving whippings
reach out grasping at hot summer air,
belying the power of the resolute vine.
Around the trunk strong, twisted stems, wrap tight
to overtake the frame on which they climb.
When summer is done pinnate leaves,
cadmium yellow, stop their twirling dance and fall.
The winter sun breaks through.

Then those who want to see will wait,
until the spring is ushered in
with the scent of purple whisperings.

Adelaide Snapshots

Cranes building soulless monoliths
behind facades of yesterday.

Windows, papered with forgotten news,
smeared with bird splats, dust, and graffiti –
lifeless eyes of empty shops, halls and churches.

A dribble of urine
trickling across the pavement
meeting a thick splash of spew
patterned with a footstep.

Abandoned cardboard, rags and plastic bottles,
left over bits of a life, filling corners –
the night abodes of invisible dossers.

Reflected in the Mall's balls
youths with tats, piercings and low-hung jeans
swaggering to a testosterone beat,
eyeing school girls with blank, black-lined eyes
sitting in jumbles,
bums on the cold pavement.

Mall spruikers' loud hype, *Shop till you drop*,
compete with preachers of doom,
urging repentance.

At the Traffic Lights

They stand at the hospital crossing.
She allows herself a second of leaning,
shadow like on his shoulder.
Cars wait until they cross.

On the footpath he walks with care,
his hand beneath her elbow.
Her steps, not even steps,
little, forward movements,
incremental eternities of going somewhere.

Her feet are thin, in flat red, rubber thongs,
her fair hair, limp,
her brittle thinness under baggy black.

He has a straw hat. She has none.
The sun beats down.

Her feet in flat, red, rubber thongs stutter forward.
Face fixed, she wills her body to stay upright.
He speaks to her, but she gives no reply.
Where is that somewhere? How far to go?
Within the thin fibres of her flesh, does she know?

He walks her with tender hope.
Her feet in flat, red, rubber thongs,
move her toward inevitable, eternal recovery.

Man with a Bare Back

He 'worked' near the busy roundabout
on a main road to the city,
every morning, for years, in all weathers.

He wore sandals and shorts, in winter a shirt
but most of the time
his copper-brown back was bare.
Plastic bags hung from his belt,
attached by some pieces of string.

His comb-over of fair hair almost covering
his bald spot, shone with a suggestion of oil.
His hazel eyes focused on footpaths
seemed intense but were missing a spark.

Leaning forward, stepping quickly, often stopping,
he collected skerricks of rubbish, and loitering leaves.
Gutter, footpath, bus stop appeared forensically clean.

Every year, the Australia Day Honours list,
posts those given gongs for community service.

What was his name?

Winter Car Park

Shopping trolleys hung with droplets,
car park full of hurrying;
shoes splashing
car tyres parting puddles,
water spraying.

A white-haired man steps out of his car.
He is tall. He stands by his car door,
looks around wondering which way to go.
He hesitates.
He waits.
He starts to walk
away
from the shopping mall.

The young bloke, who looks after the trolleys
hurries over, gently takes him by the arm,
This way, Mr Blake,
and leads the man
with a shoe on one foot,
a slipper the other,
wearing pyjama pants
and a khaki-coloured cardigan,
inside.

Lemons in Boxes

Raw light shrieks hot on dark tin roofs.
Aircons rattle in overtime.
Hundreds of grand old giants – gone.
Not many trees in gardens now,
in the tall-treed suburb of used to be.

Beneath an unremitting blue,
chainsaws shred the air.
The faithful fruit bearers – felled.
No vegie patch or lawn for play,
instead spiky plants in strict formation
guard perfect patios and pools,
in the hills-hoist gardens of used to be.

High walls hide mammoth houses;
subdivided blocks consumed.
Soft leafy entrances – lost.
Now beside hard-paved paths
white topiary roses totter on sticks,
in the birdsong gardens of used to be.

But yesterday, lemons in boxes
appeared in three streets
with signs, *Please take some*.
Childhood memories – stirred.
fruit, vegies, rabbits and fish,
often shared along my street
in the green-treed suburb of used to be.

Talk about Trees

Swimming Pool

In the end I told her.
I said, *Look, Grace, give us a break,*
if it's in the way I'll get rid of it.
I mean, we'd lived with it for fifteen years.
She hadn't whinged before, but she'd been
banging on about getting a pool for the grandkids.
I mean they don't live here and we're not swimmers.
But Grace wanted a pool.
The neighbours had a fit.
Got all fired up.
They said it was
a protected tree,
and contacted
the council.
A year ago it
was but now
the rules have
changed and
favour pro development
So we got the OK.
After all it was only a tree,
bloody thing cost me two grand to have cut down,
and I've still got to pay for the pool!

New House

G'day,
How's ya new house goin'?
Yeh, good. It's good.
What're ya neighbours like?
Well, I've only met the bloke
at the back and he's me best mate.
Why?
First coupla weeks we was here
I got rid of a big bushy tree out the back.
I'm not puttin' up with leaves, berries and bird shit.
He stuck his head over the fence and said,
Good on ya, mate.
I told him if I had my way
I'd get rid of the tree out the front.
Trouble is it's a council tree.
Maybe it'll die, mysterious like,
over summer.

A Child Asks

Dad, why are they cutting that tree down?
Excuse me, mister, my lad here wants to know
why this tree's getting the chop?
It looks pretty healthy to me.
Dad, what did he say?
Well, the man says it's in the way of the power lines
and it might drop a branch.
When will it drop a branch?
No one knows but the man said it has to go.
Did it drop a branch before?
No, not as long as I've lived here and that's forty years.
How tall is it?
Oh, about as tall as three or four houses,
one top of the other.
Is it old like Grandad?
Much older than Granddad,
I'd guess well over one hundred years.
What will happen to the animals and birds that live in it?
Dad, what will happen to them?
They'll find another tree.

Where?

Brave New Street

The start of the street was an old farm house, a
settler's cottage its end. On honeysuckle and
jasmine scented summer nights children played
on the verge, neighbours sat to chat on low brick
walls, leaned on see-through cyclone fences,
watered lawns and waited for cool gully winds.
The street belonged to everyone and everyone to it.

The farmhouse was the first to go. Overnight dull
rendered rectangles, capacious boxes smothered
blocks of land laid bare, towered over pragmatic,
post-war austerity homes, eclipsed in size, but not
in grace still standing, wide-veranda bungalows.
Then fortress front walls and corrugated fences,
instant dividers of lives and unforgiving markers
of mean spaces between houses, replaced the
friendly click of gates with private coded entry.

Clipped, calculated gardens, low trimmed hedges
ornamental pines and palms, no place for birds to
rest or nest. Under shade sails, tough plants stuck
between rocks and pebbles wither in the heat. No
dance of dappled light through leaves. No wash of
coolness under shady trees, season's rhythms,
nature's music. Residents, in bulbous SUVs, nod
to nameless neighbours. *The street belongs to no
one and no one belongs to it.*

Pie's Spot

We buried Pie
at the base of the old River Red,
where the first rays of daylight
have fallen for nearly two hundred years.
Wrapped in dad's warm wincey shirt,
she rests safely in his arms.

In the kitchen,
shopping's unpacked, the kettle's boiled,
meals are prepared, but purring Pie,
no longer part of the bustle and chat,
rests in her new spot across the lawn.

Around the garden,
butterflies flit their fleeting hours,
insects nibble through their days,
birds fly on single minded missions,
fossicking and fetching,
building nests, feeding young.

As daily cycles turn into years,
beyond those we will know
her spot will remain undisturbed,
safe in the garden she knew so well.

Staffy

He lived across the creek.
Sometimes he'd escape through the side gate.
We'd see him coming,
running low and fast over the bridge
his wagging tail propelling him on.
We'd scratch his back,
tie a rope to his collar,
walk him home.

Staffy had a woof
like his Staffordshire body
solid, strong.
Every morning his
all's well with the world woof
sounded up and down the creek.
a neighbourly reassurance.

The Fox

Vulpes vulpes

Between midnight and dawn,
with stealth, worn pads
move in silence across the oval.

A body,
following radar of whiskered directions,
skirts edges of street light pools,
shapes with walls and fences,
slips within the shadows of bushes.

Upright ears
hear earthworms wriggling in dark, damp soil,
and the tiny, far-away mouse nestling into grass.

Caught in headlights,
astute xanthic eyes change colour,
the long thick brush
stops skimming the ground,
now
straight as an arrow
balances
the body.
Swift through the black night
the urban
fox.

Victor Harbor

When taking a seaside holiday
prim maiden aunts with permed hair,
seamed stockings and sensible shoes
travelled by train to Victor.
They always stayed at the same guest house
with its large picture of the Queen,
where fine English tea was brewed in a pot
and the bone china cups were clean.
House-bare hills scrolled down to The Bluff,
holiday homes and motley shacks
clung to the curve of Encounter Bay,
where old man Rumbelow frequently fished
with his dog at the bow of his tinny.

Today as jet trails cross a summer sky
hundreds and hundreds arrive in their cars
for a break beside the sea.
On Granite Island causeway
away from the funfair's din
seagull cries and rippling waves,
slow creak of the horse-drawn tram,
thongs, bare feet, sandals and shoes
fresh rhythms on the wooden planks,
and voices from around the world
sing new songs in the cyan tide
in harmony with the summer sea's swell.

Barossa Spring

Across the valley there's a spot in time
a special space when the colours change
and winter wavers, giving way to spring.

Under morning skies, spring blue,
in traces of old orchards,
occasional trees, as if in rows
or stand-alone remnant trees,
along their dark wood branches,
thin white scatters against blue air,
almond blossoms, dancing.

The artist's hand painted them calm
distantly pastel,
Barossa paddocks, valleys and hills.

When noonday sun hints of summer's sting
in cheeky yellow, unexpected dottings
appear among grasses under grey green gums,
romp in bright light across winter paddocks
and paint hillsides with slabs of yellow:
soursobs, a contradictory weed,
a beautiful curse, so much brisk yellow
pushing past winter into the sun.

Those whose eyes saw, and whose hands planted,
knew this land would nurture
and there would be abundance.

In afternoons of amber light, avenues of palms
announce row upon row of brown bare vines,
waiting to burst in green upon their stage,
to follow timed and scripted acts:
leaf fall and bud break, flowering and fruit set,
then on to plump and colour
in the sweetening months of summer,
with harvest their finalé.

The potter's hands shaped them soft
bosoms and bottoms, motherly roundness,
the Barossa hills.

As clear sky days disappear at dusk
with chill breezes left over from winter,
across Barossa's dumpling hills
against blue back drop,
evening grey or orange sunset sky
in multitudes of yellowness, families of trees,
the ground beneath turned to gold,
around them, spring air fragrant,
the wattle, the pliant wattle,
warming winter, claiming spring.

Didgeridoo and Mukkuri Music

Japanese Cultural Day, July 2013,
Burnside Library, South Australia.
From didgeridoo comes the earth's beat,
its rhythm flows through our bodies,
from our feet on the floor,
as mystical notes of the bamboo Mukkuri
weave around and above us in afternoon air.

Together Aborigine and Ainu,
indigenous peoples playing ancestors' music,
unfolding mysteries, timeless and true,
stories of spirits, the guardians of landscape,
nature in balance, the cadence of seasons,
whispers of lovers, silk wind over grasses,
night melodies floating
over star sparkled still water,
the heavens, our heart beats,
the world's primal pulses,
our place in the universe, the past and the present,
our future with birdsong, silence or thunder,
our fears and hopes, our restless and calm.

days of green…

As a Goldfinch Sang with Clear Notes

Part 1: Meeting of friends...

Three days of sea fret, rain and icy winds,
days of slow driving, cold,
along high-hedged, narrow roads,
in a landscape perhaps magical,
there nestling in crooks and curves of valleys,
villages, glimpsed,
and running hunged between village walls
we wondered how life would be,
on a sunny Cornish day.

After these days of damp we arrived in the sun
and there was Máire, on the road,
coated, scarved and smiling warmth,
with Stephen, open-armed at the lodge door.
Our hugs embraced our children
more than half a world away.

In bunting blue the spring sun shone.
We travelled country roads and lanes,
tight squeezed between earth banks,
sides faced with stone, at their crown, hedge plants,
and at their feet, among cow parsley-lace,
gathering to celebrate the coming warm,
bright flowers: mallow, stitchwort and campion,
purple, pink, red and striking white.

Part 2: Days of green…

We entered days of green
and heard tiny birds' canticles
their song of songs
                    spring songs
                            rising above the engine.

The sun called us to fill our lungs with fresh sea air,
flowing across a land of green.
The green, that green, a green upon a thousand greens
of trees and leaves and fields,
some freckled with oxeye daisy-white
and buttercup-yellow, all within boundary walls,
marked out, and built, by generations with strong arms
and careful hands, who now by chance can still be named,
or without name returned to earth.

And here and there, canola fields of vivid yellow
or ploughed brown patches, those greens then broken,
jigsaw pieces to be placed in the coming seasons,
and so this landscape green prevails,
verdant fields, mapped by walls of stone.

Part 3: Land and sea...

along hedgerows and hill tops, in lines or
grouped, sometimes alone,
curved trees marked the prevailing wind,
their backs shaped and swept,
stoic and small,
they faced
the sun,
standing
strong:
the trees
of Cornwall.

From the lodge we watched the pheasant,
copper chested, proudly proclaiming his presence,
while, busied with pecking – his plump, brown hen
dutifully – distanced – took no notice.

Villages, dipping seaward, captured our hearts.
Cobbled streets and herringbone walls,
where in damp rock crevices, demurely in shadow,
dimpled leaves of the curious pennywort,
promising in greenish pink,
pallid spikes of bell-shaped flowers.

On the beach we held rocks rolled round
by countless tides,
lightly traced their hair-lined secrets,
scripted some ninety thousand years ago,
and pondered some mysteries of this world,
its beginning and our end.

At Kilkhampton, as eight church bells rang
on their Rogation Day, we walked through
the lychgate, followed the path
through a nicely shaggy graveyard
where among grasses bowing in breeze,
nodding English bluebells grew
tall and slender-stemmed.

We passed through the Norman doorway,
and touched carved bench ends
polished dark by five hundred years of hands
brushing past to pray:

the earth is the Lord's and everything in it…
the world and all that live in it…
and felt that we were blessed.

Part 4: A Goldfinch sang...

Then, as a goldfinch sang with clear notes
in the twilight of our evening,
the time between sunset and darkness of night,
the sun filled the horizon,
as if with mirrored light of morning
from a distant land where
kookaburras laughing, waken a new day.

Part 5: More than half a world away…

But, dear Máire, I never dreamed our friendship
would ask so much of you,
I can see you're singing glad from sad,
as the night comes when sleeping you wake,
and the day when laughing you cry…

Not a moment of a whisper
or a walk around the corner,
not a stroll across the bridge
or a few miles in the car,
not a train ride between rush hours,
or a ferry crossing channel,
not an hour or a minute,
not a moment of a whisper
but a day so long as ever,
over lands heading southward
to a place so different.

Not a moment of a whisper
or a walk around the corner,
not an unexpected drop in
to find her curled upon a chair,
not her helping hand with dinner
or her presence in the kitchen,
but knowing there are many ways
she'll show how she still cares,
and the postman brings a parcel
holding treasures she has crafted
from that place so different
more than half a world away.

Part 6: Kookaburras laughing...

And you've seen them together,
two faces on the screen.
You've heard what they've been doing,
the places they have been.
You've seen the tall caring bloke
with brown and wavy hair,
it was our son who introduced him,
now he's the one she's chosen,
and whose life she'll likely share.

Then at your snuggling down to bed
and turning off the light time,
an unexpected phone call
to tell you her day's plans,
and to wish you sweet sleeping
through the hours of your night time
as her love, a landscape green,
spans my vast and arid land.

As the goldfinch sings with clear notes
in the twilight of your evening,
kookaburras laughing, waken her new day.

from a train window...

Tides Beneath the Bridge

Japan

Between Awaji and Shikoku
beneath the Great Naruto Bridge
tides of the inland Seto Sea
meet with tides of the Pacific.

Here the swelling seas revolt,
change to a heaving mass of warring water.
Colliding and clashing, huge whirlpools,
spin, suck, sink and spew, to no avail.
In a watery hell, writhing circles
locked in an everlasting cycle.

Sailing towards Fukura port,
looking back beyond the bridge,
from sky banks of deep magnolia,
resplendent shafts of honey rich light
stretched wide across the space
where island mountains fused sea with sky,
and briefly lit a path to peace.

G8 Summit 2008, Lake Tōya

Japan

Dormant Mount Usu does not grumble,
the mountain does not smoke,
and from the middle of the lake
the lush wooded Nakajima*
invite contemplation.

In the thick and thin of air,
and the thick and thin of mist
white-edged wings pitch close to the window
red-circled eyes look in;
the flying gull, in friendship, brings
diverse perspectives to consider.
Pacific swifts sweep and glide;
slide and sift the air,
following the invisible paths of pin dot insects.

With the passing hours
flowing across the smooth and ripple,
emerging from the Nakajima woods
a distance of air, lightly dusted with dreams
falls and lifts, lifts and falls.

In the thick and thin of air,
and the thick and thin of mist.
global leaders dot and sign G8 resolutions.
Distances of air lightly dusted with dreams
fall and lift, lift and fall.

* Nakajima: island/s

Kobe Autumn Days

Japan

Clouds waterfall down valley paths
to city streets below.
Thin wisps cross autumn avenues
and somehow find the sea
to disappear, dissolve in waves
between the waiting cargo ships
in line along the wharves.

Through day and night, as clouds
converge or drift away with wind,
the lights of helipads up high
on office blocks brushing the sky
flash in and out of view.

Across the bay in swell and sway
of gusting rain and moving mists,
another city's towers rise
and claim scant space on the flat plain.

On akibare* days, when sky's intensely blue,
gleaming sun shines down glossing leaves
green-yellow, red, and orange-brown,
before they fall to ground.

And so it is, and was, and will,
Kobe's autumn days unfurl
as clouds close in, then clear.

* akibare: clear autumn sky

Autumn

France

Autumn arrives in Paris with avenues turning titian,
and fidgety winds teasing leaves
along the Boulevard St-Michel.

Well past the dwindling light of long summer days,
in short grey evenings and cold snap nights
autumn's warm colours embroider the countryside.

Poplar trees rise from carpets of ivory and amber,
veils of apricot and cinnabar screen symmetry of branches,
willows trickle bright citron over bulrushes turning brass-brown
and glory vines pattern village walls with scarlet.

Along straight Roman roads saplings,
sparse-leafed, pale-trunked and perpendicular,
stand tall against slate skies.

Nights grow longer, the keen wind cuts,
warm colours fade and fall.
Thick whey white smoke
flows from farmhouse chimneys.

Around ponds, coloured cold and still
fat grey geese, in full parade,
march with a waddle.

A plough, wood and wet iron grey,
lies idle by the gate.
The brown of newly turned earth,
the furrowed future.

Glimpses of Spring

England

After the steel chill, the long cold winter,
the season of brown, bare-limbed trees
standing stark against an empty heaven,
and days awash with ashen skies,
do not weigh me down, lift me up.
Lift me up with the colours of spring.

From bedroom windows, in honeydew light,
before night turns blue-sky day,
fresh-rinsed with spring-mist morning rain,
new buds and leaves wait for the sun.
In neighbouring gardens buffed, brimming,
bursting rich yellow, forsythia rejoicing.
Along streets from boughs low slung,
full-frothed with cherry blossoms,
falling petals sprinkle pink on grey
then quickly disappear.

Along curving country hedges
in retreating snow's brown sludge,
from frost-bleached bony grass,
green shoots begin to rise.
Over the Downs, a profusion of gorse,
carrying sunshine downhill to valleys,
passes busily bunched in hedgerows;
hawthorns, coated thick with stars, ice white.
And mirroring spring sky
across woodland floors flecked with light,
the sound of silent bluebells.

Cherry Blossoms

Japan

In a waltz with warmer days,
in timed progression,
cherry trees transform to clouds,
pure and pastel pink.
Frail blossoms faintly glow
in morning light
and day's beginnings seem luminous.

After the bleak, dismal, dim,
the strengthening sun opens wide
the possibilities of days.
People brim the streets with colour.
This is the time of hanami,*
to view the blossoms' blush
to promenade and chat with friends,
have picnics under cherry trees
and glimpse through pink tulle canopies,
white cirrus streaks on indigo.

As paper lanterns light spring nights
lovers old and new
embrace the fleeting hours of yozakura**
to whisper wishes in the dark made calm
by the hush of falling blossoms.

* hanami; cherry blossom viewing, at the beginning of spring,
reminds of the shortness and transience of life
** yozakura; night hanami

Speed Reading

A battalion of vegetables, in rows at attention,
a freshly painted back garden gate.
Flowers in beds like planted mosaics,
surround concrete statues, uninspiringly still.
Clothes on the line in orderly fashion,
pegged like with like and matching in colour.
Elegant wood piles waiting for winter.
Cover on sandpit, child's bike in the shed.

Holes in the back fence, loose palings forgotten,
morning glory slips through to tango with trees.
Wheelbarrow half full, stands in the vegie patch
overgrown with weeds.
Kaleidoscope patterns hanging on clothesline,
colours and clothes randomly pegged.
Cricket bat lying on top of the henhouse,
kid's rickety fort in a tree near the shed.

A garden hidden under a riot of rubbish,
bins overflowing, tins scattered around.
Discarded boxes and an old mattress
lying next to a ladder on yesterday's lawn.
Dog tied to a post in need of shelter…
…with rain beating down on the train window,
I stop speed reading
back gardens and private lives.

Rosebay Willow Herb

Chamerion angustifolium

Through the train window, a collage of colours,
weeds growing lush along the embankments,
each with a name, place and purpose,
each with a history, a story to tell.

Here the rosebay willow herb grows slender
and tall, tips of its stalks clustered with flowers,
surrounded by parachute seeds' white wafting filaments,
yet to be carried by wind, drop down and take root
in landscapes with shadows and scars of despair.

The train travels through cities
where it was dubbed bomb weed,
growing among ruins of World War Two
bomb sites, autumn leaves turning
from fire to blood red, and in summer,
flowers of vivid magenta,
the supposed colour of harmony,
compassion and care.

As the train passes abandoned factories,
crimson stems rising from crumbling wastelands
remind of a workforce, already forgotten,
their footsteps and voices,
recently stilled.

A Visit to Stanley

County Durham, England

Banks of daffodils lined the roads to Stanley.
Sun shone pale on gentle hills,
ewes with their lambs, grazing cows
and farm houses rising in stone from the land.
Grass covered the catacombs of closed coal mines.
Along the thread joining hills to sky,
silhouettes of wind turbines
and lacy branches of still bare trees.

In Stanley, thick haze
like smoke from distant funeral pyres,
flowed across the car park,
through the empty bus station,
shrouding public buildings, shops and pubs
with boarded-up windows,
standing shoulder to shoulder
along the Front Street Mall.

The only light an open chemist shop.
The only sound a hacking cough –
three smokers outside the Working Men's Club.
No shoppers nattering, baby's cry or child's laugh.
No colour in bare flower beds.

A few lean beings dawdled down the mall.
Near the far end, an open tea shop.
Sorry, luv, we close half three.
It was a quarter to.

O washi

Japanese, sea eagle
Haliaeetus pelagicus

She arrives every winter on giant wings,
black tipped, shoulders white,
the supreme raptor,
O washi

rides currents of air
with grace and ease,
ascends mountain peaks,
soars, circles, glides.

Revered hunter,
golden beaked and clawed,
she waits, watches, dives;

the air her engine,
the sky her domain,
the lakes and sea her table.

Come spring, on powerful wings,
she flies to her mate in Russia.
On high rock ledge or tree's strong branch
they restore and add to their aerie.

When winter returns,
again, strong wings, black-tipped, shoulders white,
will carry her south, the magnificent raptor,
O washi.

Fjord Land

Norway

Emerging from morning mists between the towering mountains,
daily ferries glide across cold fjord waters.
Smooth surface stretched before the bow mirrors walls,
rock rising sheer from watery corridors once ice.

Through the haze of morning air, in shadow,
frozen falls suspended, while those touched by the summer sun
spill water down cliffs' sculpted face to emerald bays,
some with a wooden white-spired church,
and tiny painted houses, standing neatly rowed in homage
to this land of crowning peaks.

Over the engine's steadfast throb
songs of birds in mountain trees.
Water calm, fjord deep but when the sky closes in,
and wind whips the water, lapping waves crest and trough,
the silvered stillness quickly lost, the fjord sings in minor key.

Many love this fjord land,
for it reveals the smallness of our kind.
But I need to see past low drifting clouds
filling the space huge rocks once carved at glacial pace.
Here I feel closed in and small, unable to see my way at all.

My heart lies with another place,
it too sizes down the human race:
blue-black-skied nights with chiselled stars,
and blue-day skies over red ochre sand
where fences made with wood posts and wire
skirt paddocks beyond the horizon.

**earth to earth, ashes to ashes,
dust to dust…**

Hot

Oodnadatta Track

Dust, verging on morning,
wind, scouring rust sky,
sun, scorching noontime.

In the dry drifting distance:
red sand hills
rising;

scribbled spinifex,
light tumbling
shadows;

one wind-worn post,
wood weathering grey;

splintered grass,
dead.

Summer

These are the days of a sharp sun,
north wind and shuttered windows,
dogs panting under pepper trees,
loopy flies massing in doorways,
carmine dust and smoke in the hills.

earth to earth, ashes to ashes, dust to dust…

Koalas in the Heat

Phascolarctos cinereus

They came during the worst weeks:
the air was dry, crucible dry,
the sun rose and set without birdsong,
houses throbbed under a clear fierce sky.

They came along the creek bed.
They came to our garden gate.
They were on the ground,
each hugging a tree trunk.

Over millions of years they'd evolved
to survive Australian summers.
Now they awkwardly drank the water we offered,
clumsily clutched branches we'd gathered
and looking at us with little button eyes,
chewed eucalypt leaves with anxious deliberation.

The male left.
The female stayed for many days.
Each time she saw us coming,
with urgent then calmer anticipation
she held out her large clawed paws.

I cried.

Little Grassbird

Megalurus gramineus

Across Australia on the edges of wetlands,
among tangles of lignum, sedges, tall rushes and reeds,
the little grass bird flies low, between reed beds,
blends with marsh grasses, disappears in a blink.

Above highest water mark, well hidden, dome-lidded,
a deep woven cup nest holds three pale pink eggs.
Both parents feed hatchlings, and teach them to forage;
with slender bills picking, flicking, finding marsh insects.
Their long tails stay upright, helping them balance
on slippery sedge stalks, bent rushes and reeds.

Rarely seen, seldom heard,
this tiny bird travels long distances
searching for wetlands,
almost unknown but for its clear call.

A thin call,
just three notes, *Tu peeeee, peeeee,*
carries a sadness across declining wetlands.

Is the little grassbird's cry
for the past, or the present
or for the future,
a threat to us all?

Dinner

The night sweats,
insects hover,
gecko waits on flyscreen.

Southern Sunset

Acres of sunset
mustering the night
outback Australia.

Cyclone Yasi's Reach

February 2011

Many times we'd travelled from Holbrook to Adelaide
and remembered the stretches from Oaklands to Lameroo;
long straight roads leading to an elusive horizon.

We'd seen the phantom belly dancers on bitumen,
summer's shimmering mirages, and through dust on dust
leaning out of cracked, crusty paddocks, wooden power poles
coated with dead armies of small bleached snails;
sometimes an eagle in the sky or a kookaburra on a power line,
and once, in a winter flood, water across roads and paddocks.

But on this day, ahead, above and all around,
a netherworld of raining grey.
Roads, flat wet, horizon, lost and in this muffled world,
roadside edges disappear, pools merge to lakes, link earth to sky
and everywhere but everywhere this netherworld, suffused pearl grey.

Here,
no brutal storm,
no dark clouds,
no thunder claps,
no streaks of lightning,
no change in sky, nowhere the wind,
just still trees watching sweeping plains turn inland sea.

While northern waters, vast beyond comprehension, claim lives,
full swollen Murray flows ever south-west toward the sea.
Pregnant hope of drought dry flood plains squats heavy in the air.

As blue folds over deep, pearl grey
the south awaits its day of Noah.

Evensong at Beecher's Brook

Holbrook, NSW

On the third rain day
as we sat in the evening coolness,
green-glazed gold on the north-east hills
slipped away with the settling sun,
and the creek with water,
and the busying ants,
and the birds with song,
knew.

Through the flutter of leaves
came whimsical notes of wind chimes,
and the music rose, as the tiniest twitterings
ebbed and flowed with the blue-winged banking
of circling swallows,
and fairy blue wrens skipping at garden's edge
turned high trills to arcs of song.
Magpies warbled evening vespers
over a noisy confusion of galahs
restlessly roosting in red gums.
Then, listening closely we heard,
disappearing in distance
wild shrieks from the white cockatoos,
as kookaburras laughed away the dry.

Yes
the drought had broken.

Three Gums

Keith, SA

A wide circle
of
stubbled straw
the
horizon its rim.

Treeless,
but for
three tenacious gums.

Under
a spiked sky, hot-blue
a circling hawk
dives.

The Bridge

Tooleybuc, River Murray, NSW/Victoria border

Beside the bridge sits a little park,
treed with gums, grassed in green.
From trim front gardens across the road,
summer roses stand and watch –
People come, people go over the river's bounteous flow.

Here, there was a slight, neat man,
I cannot say how old or young,
with deep-tanned face and short black hair.
He wore a stripy shirt, black suit pants
and shiny slip-on shoes.

On the path, this slight, neat man
precisely paced circles, and slowly, carefully
walked in rectangles no one else could see,
until, from a group of men near the river,
a young Hazara came and called him to the water's edge.

Far from the precipices of panic,
shrieking shells and anguished air
had he seen the lawns and trees and the roses watching?
Did he hope, one day to share this river
with those he'd left behind
in treeless mountain villages?

Was he pacing invisible maps of dusty Afghan villages
or wired perimeters, prison walls of our making?
Over the river's bounteous flow people come, people go.

ebb and flow…

Shadows

June, winter,
low sun,
late afternoon,
our long shadows stretched before us
reaching the future of our steps
before our feet.

I tried to walk into my shadow.

Burgess Hill Woman

London to Brighton, from Victoria Station

I'm in a crowded train, wondering whether
I'll be able to walk steadily when I get off.
Parkinson's medication hasn't worked well all day.

I'm sitting next to a woman,
a neat, birdlike, biscuit-brown sparrow of a woman,
with a disappearing chin, and a little pointy nose,
finger nails polished, a touch of pearl pink,
and shiny bobbed hair combed, neat, neat, neat.

Her cashmere twinset and carefully folded raincoat
harmoniously match puce-pink flowers
in her light charcoal, liberty pattern skirt.
Jet beads and smart leather shoulder bag
complete the picture.

She finishes reading,
fastidiously folds the paper,
firmly places it in the pocket above the tray table,
easily slides her mobile out of its folder
and precisely pecks a quick SMS.
After checking her watch,
effortlessly raises and secures the tray table,
deftly buttons her cardigan,
and makes ready to get off at Burgess Hill.

I bet her shoes are boring, low-heeled and grey.
I bet her stockings are flesh-coloured,
and if seams were still the fashion
I bet they'd be straight, straight, straight.

So here I am, in this crowded train
sitting next to this neat little sparrow,
who's most likely been up to London
for a day out with the girls,
whose life is probably colourless,
uneventful, but lovely,
with everything tickety boo,
who will be lucky enough to die in her sleep
after her ninety-fifth birthday,
and who, for no good reason,
I dislike immensely.

Yesterday

Yesterday
my mother died
only ten years ago,
every day I miss her,
every day I hear her
in my footsteps down the hallway,
the sound of my voice,
the things I say,
every day I see her
in the mirror.

I am older.

One December Afternoon

He was making them laugh when he died.
Had the nurses in stitches one second,
gone the next. Grandpa's death was a shock.
We didn't know cancer had crept through his body.
He was in pain, never said a word.
He'd grit his teeth as he concertinaed his tall body
into his little, blue Hillman;
drove me to and from my exams,
went into hospital the day after exams finished.
Doctor said he could attend the end of year assembly
to hear my final speech as head prefect.

I visited yesterday. I'll see him tomorrow.
Afternoon spent preparing the hall
for the junior school social.
Arrived home, found family and friends
gathered around the kitchen table
folding local newspapers.
Through tears his maiden sisters spoke in unison,
We all must carry on.
Dad's mate helped my brother deliver the papers.
Mum cooked some sort of dinner.
Nanna tried to help.
We ate.

Went to the junior school social –
duty bound.
A teacher found me crying in the toilets,
What's wrong? I couldn't answer.

Silky Oak

Mum and Dad planted one in our front garden,
I was four, my brother just born.
Soon it grew taller than the house.
Under its ballerina branches,
I'd trace the sky through fern-edged leaves
stroke their grey felt backs, and wonder why
their tops were polished like my father's shoes.
In spring, golden-orange flowers
transformed the paths and porch with pollen.
We didn't have a phone, a car or a TV.
We had the best tree in the street, a silky oak.

Dad was ill when Grandpa died.
We sold our home. We left our tree.
We moved closer to Nanna.
Dad came home for Easter,
went back to hospital and died.
I was in my teens.

Late in spring, four decades on,
when travelling from Walbundrie to Culcairn,
I saw silky oaks, standing tall among the gums,
their branches pulsing with that colour
golden-orange imbued with sun,
and felt again that part of me
which seemed to die
when I was told our tree,
had been felled before its time.

Briefcase

Dug out from the back of the wardrobe,
a leather case, chestnut brown.
Felt smooth. Smelt good.
Its mended edges sewn with different sorts of string.

Inside, stuck on the lid, an improvised pocket
made from embroidered furniture fabric.
The cavity lined with stick-on plastic,
the stuff used for covering school books,
purple with a bronze pattern.

Couldn't shut it.
Couldn't use it.
Consigned to the culling pile.

The case, travelled with him every day, on his pushbike,
then in his first car, a Morris Oxford.
He'd park under the Moreton Bay fig trees,
near the Torrens weir, and walk to work.
He'd say a daily prayer as he crossed Morphett Street Bridge,
continued on past Holy Trinity, where he'd been married,
until he reached the big oak doors of Goldsborough Mort.

To keep working he downgraded jobs several times.
The case went with him to cement works at Birkenhead;
Highways Department at Pooraka;
Enfield City Council on Regency Road.

It's back in the wardrobe.
When I'm gone, it can go too.
Dad died aged forty-six.

Today's Tide

Today's tide
brings yesterday's splinters of experience,
smoothed and bleached by wind and sand years.
Old pieces of driftwood,
memories tempered more gently.
Calm in their presence I follow waves' endings.
With time the ebb and flow will change
the sharp-edged
now.

My Humbling Days

What will I say in my humbling days
when I am called to account,
and find my past is a memory
of lost opportunities,
an accumulation of ordinary moments
forever wasted or wished away:
frazzled seconds at traffic lights;
impatient moments at checkouts;
minutes spent sublimating surges
of exasperation or boredom,
For Pete's sake, shut up!
Get on with the story.
Finish the sentence;
flashes of finger-tapping frustration
while waiting,
with my bum parked on a hard seat
My appointment was for 10.
It's now past 11;
or despondent mornings,
believing the pattern of my day was set
filling the hours with busy nothingness,
a mouse, treading a wheel, going nowhere;
and times of dejection,
wishing myself in someone else's skin,
resigned to that feeling of cold
arriving just after sunset ?

Horizon Line

Early that mild spring morning
a sun of jonquil yellow
shone through the hospital window.

Her family stood beside the bed,
in the corner of the ward,
in a patch of sunlight.

Down the road lay the pebbled beach.
Rippling waves reached the shore,
shimmered, bubbled, disappeared.

As circling seagulls gave up their cries
and flew out over a silver sea,
a small boat slipped anchor
and set sail for the horizon.

The Forest

Kuitpo

Along pine-needle-padded paths
in filtered green with shafts of gold,
between the tall and taller pines
down empty aisles of silence,
collecting pine cones, we walked
toward the far off sunlight.

High up, tree tips touched by the light,
below, mossed trunks of fallen trees,
first thought as sombre, dead and dark.

Above my breath, and beating heart,
I heard the faintest songs of trees
and felt a new-found strength,
a sense of something great and good
in this gilded green cathedral.

Author's note

Since I retired, writing poetry has helped me lose myself in a world away from the daily challenges of Parkinson's disease. I've always made notes to remember people and places. I kept years of scribbles in an old explosives box. They emerged from the box in late 2011, not as an explosion but more as a catalyst for my timely venture into poetry.

Foundation

My longest friendships reach back 64 years and I have many friends in close and wider circles but the natural world has always been my best friend. As a child, I spent many hours gardening with my parents and grandparents. I remember encouraging the flowers, fruit and vegetables to grow. I loved watching birds and other creatures. For me, gardens were places of perfume, mystery, renewal and at times a calming refuge. When Dad bought a car, I relished our weekend trips to 'big gardens', namely the hills or the beach. These trips gave my brother and me the chance to explore the wide world and to go crabbing, mushrooming and blackberry picking.

I think my love of words and poetry came from a number of sources. I was an avid reader. My Nanna's stories enthralled me. I studied elocution with one of my paternal great-aunts. I remember feeling the sounds of words in my mouth. I liked being on stage. My family attended church and I enjoyed the music of words in Bible readings.

As a child, I was intrigued when my maternal aunt would suddenly swap from English to German to name something or quote a favourite saying. Recently I learned that my maternal ancestors, farmers of German descent, arrived from Prussia (now part of Poland) between 1838 and 1859 and were among the first settlers in Hahndorf in the Mount Lofty Ranges, and Hoffnungsthal near Lyndoch in the Barossa Valley.

My paternal ancestors, market gardeners, teachers and tradesmen, came from several counties across England between 1847 and 1865 and settled in Nairne, Kapunda, Piccadilly Valley and in North Adelaide and Kensington.

Framework

My primary school teachers, Ms O'Loughlin and Ms Sweet, and secondary school teachers, Mrs Wilkins and Mrs Ely, developed my interest in poetry and the power of words. I furthered my understanding of English, as a complex and richly expressive language, while studying English Literature at the University of Adelaide.

I first taught at Gepps Cross Girls High School, and then went to Morialta High School in its inaugural year. From there I went on to establish the Languages and Multicultural Library in Grote Street, Adelaide. I spent the rest of my career in a number of teaching and leadership roles within the English as a Second Language and New Arrivals programs.

Bricks

In my 67 years I have been blessed with a loving family, good friends and colleagues; received a debt-free university education and travelled in Australia and overseas. I met my future husband, from Brighton, England, on a plane to Russia in 1976. Thanks to my mother, I juggled raising a family with a career. Two remarkable boys and their equally remarkable partners continue to bring much joy, as does our baby granddaughter. I live in a democratic, civil society, a very liveable city and a breathtaking ancient land. I have the luxury of time in retirement to write poetry.

Mortar

Thanks to my friends Joan Richards, Deb Bryant, Connie Leach, Máire and Catherine Kite, Hilary Marshall and, from the Lyceum Club, Adelaide, Helen Carey.

Thanks to poet Professor Jeri Kroll, Flinders University, for looking at some of my early poems and suggesting I join Friendly Street Poets.

Thanks to poets at Friendly Street for their encouragement, particularly Elaine Barker, co-editor of *Reader 37*, for publishing the first poem I read at FSP; Martin Christmas, for his feedback and photographs; Erica Jolly, for making my day when she said, in her distinct Erica voice, 'I like your poems. They've got guts.' Erica introduced me to Graham Rowlands, who gently but firmly guided me with his red biro incisive comments and jewels of praise. Louise Nicholas encouraged me to publish and introduced me to Jude Aquilina, with whom I received an Arts SA Richard Llewellyn Arts & Disability Emerging Artist Mentorship grant in 2014. Jude, always enthusiastic and caring, gained an overview of my poems, suggested some changes and worked with me, after the grant had finished, to put together *Nudge the Morning*.

And thanks to my family, for keeping me grounded. Alan, upon finding himself alone in the lounge room, would jokingly remark, 'You doing poetry again?' He has ferried me to and fro and, when asked, provided a pragmatic opinion. My granddaughter, Madeleine, has inspired me to keep on writing.